This Baptism Guest Book Belongs to

_____

 My *Baptism* Wishes for You

I HOPE YOU

Are Never Afraid of...

Ignore...

Become...

Never Forget...

Love...

Create...

Find...

Learn...

Accept...

Laugh...

Live...

With Love, From

. . . .

My Baptism Wishes for You

I HOPE YOU

Are Never Afraid of...

Ignore...

Become...

Never Forget...

Love...

Create...

Find...

Learn...

Accept...

Laugh...

Live...

With Love, From

. . . .

 My Baptism Wishes for You

I HOPE YOU

Are Never Afraid of...

Ignore...

Become...

Never Forget...

Love...

Create...

Find...

Learn...

Accept...

Laugh...

Live...

With Love, From

. . . .

 My Baptism Wishes for You

I HOPE YOU

Are Never Afraid of...

Ignore...

Become...

Never Forget...

Love...

Create...

Find...

Learn...

Accept...

Laugh...

Live...

With Love, From

. . . .

 My Baptism Wishes for You

I HOPE YOU

Are Never Afraid of...

Ignore...

Become...

Never Forget...

Love...

Create...

Find...

Learn...

Accept...

Laugh...

Live...

With Love, From

. . . .

 My Baptism Wishes for You

I HOPE YOU

Are Never Afraid of...

Ignore...

Become...

Never Forget...

Love...

Create...

Find...

Learn...

Accept...

Laugh...

Live...

With Love, From

· · · · · · · · · · · · · · · · · · ·

My Baptism Wishes for You

I HOPE YOU

Are Never Afraid of...

Ignore...

Become...

Never Forget...

Love...

Create...

Find...

Learn...

Accept...

Laugh...

Live...

With Love, From

 My Baptism Wishes for You

I HOPE YOU

Are Never Afraid of...

Ignore...

Become...

Never Forget...

Love...

Create...

Find...

Learn...

Accept...

Laugh...

Live...

With Love, From

· · · · · · · · · · · · · · · · · · · ·

 My Baptism Wishes for You

I HOPE YOU

Are Never Afraid of...

Ignore...

Become...

Never Forget...

Love...

Create...

Find...

Learn...

Accept...

Laugh...

Live...

With Love, From

. . . .

 "God sometimes takes us into troubled waters not to drown us but to cleanse us."

My Baptism Wishes for You

I HOPE YOU

Are Never Afraid of...

_____

Ignore...

_____

Become...

_____

Never Forget...

_____

Love...

_____

Create...

_____

Find...

_____

Learn...

_____

Accept...

_____

Laugh...

_____

Live...

_____

With Love, From

· ·

 My Baptism Wishes for You

I HOPE YOU

Are Never Afraid of...

Ignore...

Become...

Never Forget...

Love...

Create...

Find...

Learn...

Accept...

Laugh...

Live...

With Love, From

. . . .

 My Baptism Wishes for You

I HOPE YOU

Are Never Afraid of...

Ignore...

Become...

Never Forget...

Love...

Create...

Find...

Learn...

Accept...

Laugh...

Live...

With Love, From

· ·

 My Baptism Wishes for You

I HOPE YOU

Are Never Afraid of...

Ignore...

Become...

Never Forget...

Love...

Create...

Find...

Learn...

Accept...

Laugh...

Live...

With Love, From

· · · · · · · · · · · · · · · · · · · ·

 My Baptism Wishes for You

I HOPE YOU

Are Never Afraid of...

Ignore...

Become...

Never Forget...

Love...

Create...

Find...

Learn...

Accept...

Laugh...

Live...

With Love, From

. . . .

 My Baptism Wishes for You

I HOPE YOU

Are Never Afraid of...
_____

Ignore...
_____

Become...
_____

Never Forget...
_____

Love...
_____

Create...
_____

Find...
_____

Learn...
_____

Accept...
_____

Laugh...
_____

Live...
_____

With Love, From

· · · · · · · · · · · · · · · · · · · ·

My Baptism Wishes for You

I HOPE YOU

Are Never Afraid of...

Ignore...

Become...

Never Forget...

Love...

Create...

Find...

Learn...

Accept...

Laugh...

Live...

With Love, From

My Baptism Wishes for You

I HOPE YOU

Are Never Afraid of...

Ignore...

Become...

Never Forget...

Love...

Create...

Find...

Learn...

Accept...

Laugh...

Live...

With Love, From

· ·

 My *Baptism* Wishes for You

I HOPE YOU

Are Never Afraid of...

Ignore...

Become...

Never Forget...

Love...

Create...

Find...

Learn...

Accept...

Laugh...

Live...

With Love, From

 My Baptism Wishes for You

I HOPE YOU

Are Never Afraid of...

Ignore...

Become...

Never Forget...

Love...

Create...

Find...

Learn...

Accept...

Laugh...

Live...

With Love, From

 My Baptism Wishes for You

I HOPE YOU

Are Never Afraid of...

Ignore...

Become...

Never Forget...

Love...

Create...

Find...

Learn...

Accept...

Laugh...

Live...

With Love, From

 "Blessed are those who have not seen him and yet believe." –John 20:29

 My Baptism Wishes for You

I HOPE YOU

Are Never Afraid of...

Ignore...

Become...

Never Forget...

Love...

Create...

Find...

Learn...

Accept...

Laugh...

Live...

With Love, From

 My Baptism Wishes for You

I HOPE YOU

Are Never Afraid of...

Ignore...

Become...

Never Forget...

Love...

Create...

Find...

Learn...

Accept...

Laugh...

Live...

With Love, From

· · · · · · · · · · · · · · · · · · ·

 My Baptism Wishes for You

I HOPE YOU

Are Never Afraid of...

Ignore...

Become...

Never Forget...

Love...

Create...

Find...

Learn...

Accept...

Laugh...

Live...

With Love, From

. . . .

 My Baptism Wishes for You

I HOPE YOU

Are Never Afraid of...

Ignore...

Become...

Never Forget...

Love...

Create...

Find...

Learn...

Accept...

Laugh...

Live...

With Love, From

. . . .

 My Baptism Wishes for You

I HOPE YOU

Are Never Afraid of...
_____

Ignore...
_____

Become...
_____

Never Forget...
_____

Love...
_____

Create...
_____

Find...
_____

Learn...
_____

Accept...
_____

Laugh...
_____

Live...
_____

With Love, From

. . . .

 My Baptism Wishes for You

I HOPE YOU

Are Never Afraid of...

Ignore...

Become...

Never Forget...

Love...

Create...

Find...

Learn...

Accept...

Laugh...

Live...

With Love, From

· ·

 My Baptism Wishes for You

I HOPE YOU

Are Never Afraid of...

Ignore...

Become...

Never Forget...

Love...

Create...

Find...

Learn...

Accept...

Laugh...

Live...

With Love, From

· · · · · · · · · · · · · · · · · · · ·

 My Baptism Wishes for You

I HOPE YOU

Are Never Afraid of...

Ignore...

Become...

Never Forget...

Love...

Create...

Find...

Learn...

Accept...

Laugh...

Live...

With Love, From

. . . .

 My Baptism Wishes for You

I HOPE YOU

Are Never Afraid of...

Ignore...

Become...

Never Forget...

Love...

Create...

Find...

Learn...

Accept...

Laugh...

Live...

With Love, From

. . . .

 My Baptism Wishes for You

I HOPE YOU

Are Never Afraid of...

Ignore...

Become...

Never Forget...

Love...

Create...

Find...

Learn...

Accept...

Laugh...

Live...

With Love, From

 "For you are God's masterpiece created in Christ to do good works which God prepared in advance for you to do."

 My Baptism Wishes for You

I HOPE YOU

Are Never Afraid of...

Ignore...

Become...

Never Forget...

Love...

Create...

Find...

Learn...

Accept...

Laugh...

Live...

With Love, From

· ·

 My *Baptism Wishes for You*

I HOPE YOU

Are Never Afraid of...

Ignore...

Become...

Never Forget...

Love...

Create...

Find...

Learn...

Accept...

Laugh...

Live...

With Love, From

· · · · · · · · · · · · · · · · · · ·

 My Baptism Wishes for You

I HOPE YOU

Are Never Afraid of...

Ignore...

Become...

Never Forget...

Love...

Create...

Find...

Learn...

Accept...

Laugh...

Live...

With Love, From

. . . .

My Baptism Wishes for You

I HOPE YOU

Are Never Afraid of...

Ignore...

Become...

Never Forget...

Love...

Create...

Find...

Learn...

Accept...

Laugh...

Live...

With Love, From

. . . .

 My Baptism Wishes for You

I HOPE YOU

Are Never Afraid of...

Ignore...

Become...

Never Forget...

Love...

Create...

Find...

Learn...

Accept...

Laugh...

Live...

With Love, From

. . . .

My Baptism Wishes for You

I HOPE YOU

Are Never Afraid of...

Ignore...

Become...

Never Forget...

Love...

Create...

Find...

Learn...

Accept...

Laugh...

Live...

With Love, From

· · · · · · · · · · · · · · · · · · · ·

 My Baptism Wishes for You

I HOPE YOU

Are Never Afraid of...

Ignore...

Become...

Never Forget...

Love...

Create...

Find...

Learn...

Accept...

Laugh...

Live...

With Love, From

. . . .

 My *Baptism Wishes for You*

I HOPE YOU

Are Never Afraid of...

Ignore...

Become...

Never Forget...

Love...

Create...

Find...

Learn...

Accept...

Laugh...

Live...

With Love, From

 My Baptism Wishes for You

I HOPE YOU

Are Never Afraid of...

Ignore...

Become...

Never Forget...

Love...

Create...

Find...

Learn...

Accept...

Laugh...

Live...

With Love, From

. . . .

 My Baptism Wishes for You

I HOPE YOU

Are Never Afraid of...

Ignore...

Become...

Never Forget...

Love...

Create...

Find...

Learn...

Accept...

Laugh...

Live...

With Love, From

. . . .

 "*I can do all things through Christ
who strengthens me.*"
-*Philippians 4:13*

 My Baptism Wishes for You

I HOPE YOU

Are Never Afraid of...

Ignore...

Become...

Never Forget...

Love...

Create...

Find...

Learn...

Accept...

Laugh...

Live...

With Love, From

. . . .

 My Baptism Wishes for You

I HOPE YOU

Are Never Afraid of...

Ignore...

Become...

Never Forget...

Love...

Create...

Find...

Learn...

Accept...

Laugh...

Live...

With Love, From

· ·

 My Baptism Wishes for You

I HOPE YOU

Are Never Afraid of...

Ignore...

Become...

Never Forget...

Love...

Create...

Find...

Learn...

Accept...

Laugh...

Live...

With Love, From

. . . .

 My Baptism Wishes for You

I HOPE YOU

Are Never Afraid of...

Ignore...

Become...

Never Forget...

Love...

Create...

Find...

Learn...

Accept...

Laugh...

Live...

With Love, From

. . . .

My Baptism Wishes for You

I HOPE YOU

Are Never Afraid of...

Ignore...

Become...

Never Forget...

Love...

Create...

Find...

Learn...

Accept...

Laugh...

Live...

With Love, From

. . . .

 My Baptism Wishes for You

I HOPE YOU

Are Never Afraid of...

Ignore...

Become...

Never Forget...

Love...

Create...

Find...

Learn...

Accept...

Laugh...

Live...

With Love, From

. . . .

My Baptism Wishes for You

I HOPE YOU

Are Never Afraid of...

Ignore...

Become...

Never Forget...

Love...

Create...

Find...

Learn...

Accept...

Laugh...

Live...

With Love, From

. . . .

 My Baptism Wishes for You

I HOPE YOU

Are Never Afraid of...

Ignore...

Become...

Never Forget...

Love...

Create...

Find...

Learn...

Accept...

Laugh...

Live...

With Love, From

. . . .

 My *Baptism Wishes for You*

I HOPE YOU

Are Never Afraid of...

Ignore...

Become...

Never Forget...

Love...

Create...

Find...

Learn...

Accept...

Laugh...

Live...

With Love, From

. . . .

My Baptism Wishes for You

I HOPE YOU

Are Never Afraid of...

Ignore...

Become...

Never Forget...

Love...

Create...

Find...

Learn...

Accept...

Laugh...

Live...

With Love, From

. . . .

 "There are times when we have to step into the darkness in faith, confident that God will place solid ground beneath our feet once we do."

 My Baptism Wishes for You

I HOPE YOU

Are Never Afraid of...

Ignore...

Become...

Never Forget...

Love...

Create...

Find...

Learn...

Accept...

Laugh...

Live...

With Love, From

. . . .

My Baptism Wishes for You

I HOPE YOU

Are Never Afraid of...

Ignore...

Become...

Never Forget...

Love...

Create...

Find...

Learn...

Accept...

Laugh...

Live...

With Love, From

· ·

My Baptism Wishes for You

I HOPE YOU

Are Never Afraid of...

Ignore...

Become...

Never Forget...

Love...

Create...

Find...

Learn...

Accept...

Laugh...

Live...

With Love, From

. . . .

 My *Baptism Wishes for You*

I HOPE YOU

Are Never Afraid of...

Ignore...

Become...

Never Forget...

Love...

Create...

Find...

Learn...

Accept...

Laugh...

Live...

With Love, From

· · · · · · · · · · · · · · · · · · · ·

My Baptism Wishes for You

I HOPE YOU

Are Never Afraid of...

Ignore...

Become...

Never Forget...

Love...

Create...

Find...

Learn...

Accept...

Laugh...

Live...

With Love, From

 My Baptism Wishes for You

I HOPE YOU

Are Never Afraid of...

Ignore...

Become...

Never Forget...

Love...

Create...

Find...

Learn...

Accept...

Laugh...

Live...

With Love, From

 My Baptism Wishes for You

I HOPE YOU

Are Never Afraid of...

Ignore...

Become...

Never Forget...

Love...

Create...

Find...

Learn...

Accept...

Laugh...

Live...

With Love, From

 My Baptism Wishes for You

I HOPE YOU

Are Never Afraid of...

Ignore...

Become...

Never Forget...

Love...

Create...

Find...

Learn...

Accept...

Laugh...

Live...

With Love, From

. . . .

 My Baptism Wishes for You

I HOPE YOU

Are Never Afraid of...

Ignore...

Become...

Never Forget...

Love...

Create...

Find...

Learn...

Accept...

Laugh...

Live...

With Love, From

· ·

My Baptism Wishes for You

I HOPE YOU

Are Never Afraid of...

Ignore...

Become...

Never Forget...

Love...

Create...

Find...

Learn...

Accept...

Laugh...

Live...

With Love, From

. . . .

 "Don't shine so others can see you.
Shine so that through you, others can
see him."

My Baptism Wishes for You

I HOPE YOU

Are Never Afraid of...

Ignore...

Become...

Never Forget...

Love...

Create...

Find...

Learn...

Accept...

Laugh...

Live...

With Love, From

. . . .

 My Baptism Wishes for You

I HOPE YOU

Are Never Afraid of...

Ignore...

Become...

Never Forget...

Love...

Create...

Find...

Learn...

Accept...

Laugh...

Live...

With Love, From

. . . .

 My Baptism Wishes for You

I HOPE YOU

Are Never Afraid of...

Ignore...

Become...

Never Forget...

Love...

Create...

Find...

Learn...

Accept...

Laugh...

Live...

With Love, From

. . . .

 My Baptism Wishes for You

I HOPE YOU

Are Never Afraid of...

Ignore...

Become...

Never Forget...

Love...

Create...

Find...

Learn...

Accept...

Laugh...

Live...

With Love, From

. . . .

 My Baptism Wishes for You

I HOPE YOU

Are Never Afraid of...

Ignore...

Become...

Never Forget...

Love...

Create...

Find...

Learn...

Accept...

Laugh...

Live...

With Love, From

. . . .

 *My Baptism Wishes for You*

I HOPE YOU

Are Never Afraid of...

Ignore...

Become...

Never Forget...

Love...

Create...

Find...

Learn...

Accept...

Laugh...

Live...

With Love, From

. . . .

 My Baptism Wishes for You

I HOPE YOU

Are Never Afraid of...

Ignore...

Become...

Never Forget...

Love...

Create...

Find...

Learn...

Accept...

Laugh...

Live...

With Love, From

. . . .

 My Baptism Wishes for You

I HOPE YOU

Are Never Afraid of...

Ignore...

Become...

Never Forget...

Love...

Create...

Find...

Learn...

Accept...

Laugh...

Live...

With Love, From

. . . .

 My Baptism Wishes for You

I HOPE YOU

Are Never Afraid of...

Ignore...

Become...

Never Forget...

Love...

Create...

Find...

Learn...

Accept...

Laugh...

Live...

With Love, From

. . . .

 My *Baptism Wishes for You*

I HOPE YOU

Are Never Afraid of...

Ignore...

Become...

Never Forget...

Love...

Create...

Find...

Learn...

Accept...

Laugh...

Live...

With Love, From

"*The lord is my strength and my shield.*"

–Psalms 28:7

Made in the USA
Monee, IL
20 July 2021